Little Scientists, BIG Questions

What Does a Chocolate Maker Do?

Written by Ruth Owen and Designed by Alix Wood

WINDMILL BOOKS

Published in 2025 by Windmill Books,
an Imprint of Rosen Publishing
2544 Clinton St.
Buffalo, NY 14224

Cataloging-in-Publication Data

Names: Owen, Ruth.
Title: What does a chocolate maker do? / Ruth Owen.
Description: Buffalo, New York : Windmill Books, 2025. | Series: Little scientists, big questions
Identifiers: ISBN 9781538395455 (pbk.) | ISBN 9781538395462 (library bound) | ISBN 9781538395479 (ebook)
Subjects: LCSH: Food engineers--Juvenile literature. | Food science--Juvenile literature. | Food industry and trade--Technological innovations--Juvenile literature.
Classification: LCC TP369.5 O94 2025 | DDC 664.0092--dc23

Image Credits:
Alamy: 14 (Jeff Gilbert), 17T (dpa picture alliance archive); Ruby Tuesday Books: 7TR; Shutterstock: Cover (Marcos Castillo), 4 (Ivonne Wierink/Lanlana839/Chones/Crepesoles), 5 (rocharibeiro), 6 (Kaisarmuda), 7L (Media Lens King), 8 (tristan tan), 9T (Kaiskynet Studio), 9B (no borders – Brayden Howie), 10L (mavo), 10R (Photoongraphy), 11T (EshanaPhoto), 11B (Africa Studio), 12 (Evgeny Haritonov), 13T (Serge Yatunin), 13C (MaraZe/Valentin Valkov), 13B (baibaz), 15T (Hekla), 15B (Javier Volcan), 17B (xpixel), 18T (Hydr Ercn), 18B (LightField Studios), 19 (Tim UR/panuwat panyacharoen/AmyLv/LN team/ Maks Narodenk ... Alfio/boommaval/Food Impressions/Ho ... 20TL (wavebreakme ... (Allen.G), 22TL ... 23T (irin-k), 23

Printed in

CPSIA Compliance

For Further Information contact Rosen Publishing

I0807143

Find us on

What is YOUR favorite food?

I like sweet, juicy grapes.

Our favorite treat is YUMMY chocolate!

People eat chocolate in lots of different ways.

Easter eggs

Fancy chocolates

Chocolate bar

Did you know that chocolate comes from trees?

Chocolate chips in cookies

Chocolate is made from seeds that grow on a cacao tree.

Let's say it! "kuh-KOW"

How does a chocolate maker use science to turn seeds into chocolate?

Come on, little scientists, let's answer that BIG question!

The science of making chocolate begins with a farmer.

Farmers in parts of South America, Africa, and Asia grow cacao trees.

The trees need hot weather and lots of rain.

Get ready for some BIG science!

A cacao tree grows tiny, tiny flowers.

Next, mini flies called midges zoom from flower to flower carrying pollen.

The tiny flowers grow big pods filled with seeds which the farmers collect.

Without the tiny flies there would be no chocolate!

Inside each cacao pod there are up to 50 seeds.

The white stuff is called pulp.

Chocolate makers call the seeds cacao, or cocoa, beans.

The cocoa beans and pulp are put into boxes.

Inside the box, the beans start to warm up and ferment.

- Fermenting kills germs.
- It makes the beans' shells get softer.
- The beans' taste gets better too!

Cocoa beans and pulp

Drying beans

Finally, the beans are dried in hot sunshine.

The dried beans may travel thousands of miles on a ship to a chocolate factory.

Then the chocolate makers get to work with science and special machines!

First, the beans are roasted in an oven.

Next, another machine removes the beans' shells.

Soon, all that's left are tiny bits of cocoa, called cocoa nibs.

Next, the chocolate maker puts the solid cocoa nibs into a grinding machine.

The wheels of the machine grind and crush the nibs against a big stone at the bottom of the machine.

The grinding also causes friction, which makes heat.

Try rubbing your hands together fast. They get hot because of friction.

The grinding and heat change the solid nibs into a thick, smooth liquid.

The chocolate maker adds ingredients to the liquid.

Sugar

Milk powder

Vanilla

Dark chocolate

Little to no milk powder

Milk chocolate

More milk powder

Get ready for more BIG science!

Now the chocolate maker tempers the liquid chocolate by heating and then cooling it.

Sometimes they do this by spreading the hot liquid chocolate onto a cold, stone counter.

When the chocolate's temperature is just right, it is ready.

Tempered chocolate looks shiny. It stays hard and snaps when you break it.

Tempered chocolate bar

Chocolate that has not been tempered is bendy, crumbly, and dull.

Untempered chocolate bar

At the chocolate factory, the liquid tempered chocolate is poured into molds.

The liquid chocolate takes the shape of the hollow mold.

The molds are tapped on a hard surface to burst any air bubbles in the chocolate.

The chocolate goes into a refrigerator to cool.

As it cools, chocolate turns solid. Then it's removed from the molds.

The chocolate is wrapped in foil paper to keep it fresh.

Some chocolate makers are called chocolatiers.

A chocolatier works in a special kitchen.

Let's say it! "sho-kuh-lah-TEERZ"

They invent new ways to eat this treat.

Chocolatiers try mixing different ingredients with chocolate to create new flavors.

Coconut

Fruit

Nuts

Spicy peppercorns

Hot chilies

Peppermint leaves

Flowers

Seaweed

Moss

Berries

Roasted garlic

Chocolatiers make paints that we can eat to decorate chocolates.

Sweet-tasting paint

They put yummy ingredients inside chocolates.

Painted chocolates

Chocolatiers use molds to make special chocolate sculptures, or models.

Sometimes they carve large lumps of chocolate into sculptures.

Chocolate elephant sculpture

Let's check out some BIG chocolate science again!

Crushing cocoa nibs and melting them with heat turns them from a **solid** into a **liquid**.

Solid

Liquid

When liquid chocolate cools, it becomes solid again.

And if we leave chocolate in hot sunshine, it melts and turns to liquid again!

A chocolate maker is a cook, an inventor, AND a scientist!

Now we know how chocolate makers use science.

Good work, little scientists!

My Science Words

ferment
To change through a special chemical breakdown so that a substance has a different taste.

friction
A force that resists motion when one object moves over another.

ingredients
Different foods that can be mixed to make another type of food.

mold
A hollow, or empty, container in a special shape. When a substance in the mold turns solid, the substance takes the mold's shape.